AF327799

SOUTHERN CALIFORNIA AT THE TURN OF THE CENTURY

Edited by Graham Mackintosh

Descriptive Text by Major Ben C. Truman

Ross-Erikson   Santa Barbara   1977

ROSS-ERIKSON, INC. PUBLISHERS
223 Via Sevilla
Santa Barbara, Ca. 93109 USA

SOUTHERN CALIFORNIA BEFORE THE AUTOMOBILE

This little book was published first in 1900 not in Southern California, but in Philadelphia. Its circulation was, as far as can be determined, largely in the East, with the intent of getting in on the very real curiosity the rest of the country had about that exotic land next to the Pacific where oranges grew on Joshua trees and the seasons never changed. One presumes also that discouraging words were seldom heard; certainly the introduction by Major Ben C. Truman contains none. In fact his language is so encouraging we can do no more than reproduce it here as a running text.

With that, then, let us enter . . .

That part of California lying south and east of Point Concepcion on the ocean and west of the

Coast range of mountains, embracing Santa Barbara, Ventura, Los Angeles, Orange,

San Bernardino, Riverside and San Diego Counties, is geographically and prominently known

as Southern California — and sometimes as "Semi-Tropical California," on account of its being

the natural home of the lemon, the orange, the citron, the pomegranate, the guava and the fig.

The Mount Lowe Railway incline.

By a peculiar configuration of nearly two hundred miles of mountains at a distance of from

thirty to ninety miles from a warm sunny sea, with detached and other spurs reaching out from

the mother range in various directions and sometimes abutting the sea, there has been created

a land such as exists nowhere else in the world—where there are no excessive heats and

no uncomfortable colds; neither pronounced summer nor pronounced winter; where for the

San Gabriel Mission, near Los Angeles.

entire year there exists that delightful interlude known in the east, or elsewhere than in the

section being described, as Indian Summer; where flowers bloom and grasses lengthen and

fruits ripen every week in the year, and where the green pea and the strawberry—those two

nobles of the garden—may be picked and served every month from January to December;

where no snows, no freezing, no sunstrokes and no disastrous winds have ever been recorded,

and where there are so many blandishments and other enticements of climate and of

healthfulness and soil that it has become known throughout the remotest part of the United

States as the gem spot of the world.   The whole of Southern California forms a panorama

such as exists nowhere else on the globe, and is spread over with beautiful and thriving cities

and towns, orange groves and vineyards, and thousands of magnificent homes of the cultivated

and wealthy from all parts of the United States, while there are mountain resorts, and island

and other seaside resorts innumerable. Go where you may throughout this favored section and

Panoramic view of Redlands from Smiley Heights.

you will see thousands of homes festooned in flowers the year round and surrounded by orange

and lemon trees, from which fruit is picked every day in the calendar, and where the mockbird,

the linnet and the thrush mingle their melodies with the fragrant spices and sweets from

flower and herb.   There is a flavor of romance about orange growing that captivates

seekers after occidental homes. It strikes them as the most fascinating of all the occupations

of husbandry, where there is enticing labor among perennial verdure and fragrant blossoms

which are supposed to produce a bountiful harvest of doubly golden fruit. The habitat of the

orange is suggestive of a good rich soil and of a semi-tropical climate. And while the young tree

is coy and sometimes wayward and requires intelligent and affectionate caressing, it is neither

difficult to manage nor abstruse in the theories which make it an appreciative and profitable

pet.　　　When all things are considered, therefore, Southern California is by far the most

beautiful and generally attractive section of country in the world, and is so pronounced by all.

Its system of railroads far surpass those of San Francisco or any other city of the Pacific Coast.

Its electric street railways have much more mileage than any other city of its size in any

country. And nearly as much may be said of all the fine cities of this remarkable Southern

California country. San Diego and its interior valleys and hillsides are the most desirable

places even in California for people suffering from pulmonary, neuralgic and many other

complaints. Her mountains abound in pine groves and ice-cold springs of crystal water and her

sea breezes are delicious beyond description. Pasadena, Redlands and Riverside are gems

that carry ecstasy to all hearts. And Santa Barbara—that pearl of a place—boasts a climate

so salubrious and so delightful, and a situation so enchanting, as to make all other places

jealous of its irresistible charms. And then there is that entrancing island of Santa Catalina,

less than thirty miles from San Pedro, whose witchery of situation and loveliness of clime

On the beach, Santa Monica.

constitute a veritable Vallambrosa, where the seeker after health or rest or piscatorial

adventure revels in his ideal.